GLOBETROTTERS

INDONESIA

Jane Hinchey

REDBACK publishing

First Published 2023 by
Redback Publishing
PO Box 357 Frenchs Forest NSW 2086
Australia

www.redbackpublishing.com
orders@redbackpublishing.com

ISBN 978-1-76140-030-8 PBK

Author: Jane Hinchey
Editor: Marlene Vaughan
Design: Redback Publishing

Original illustrations © Redback Publishing 2023
Originated by Redback Publishing

Acknowledgements
Abbreviations: l–left, r–right, b–bottom, t–top, c–centre, m–middle
We would like to thank the following for permission to reproduce photographs:
(Images © shutterstock, wikimediacommons)
p7tl Katiekk, p8tl Akhmad Dody Firmansyah, p8tr Akhmad Dody Firmansyah, p9tl Hariandi Hafid, p9tr Adi Haririe, p9bc Dede Sudiana, p11tr Eva Afifah, p11cr Paulharding00, p12tl INDONESIAPIX, p12br kalilipatvideoart, p13tr raditya, p13bl Sony Herdiana, p14cr Bastian AS, p14bl AMRUL AZUAR MOKHTAR, p15cl Sony Herdiana, p16br Shalstock, p18br Dolly MJ, p19tl Sudarsani Ida Ayu Putu, p19br Marius Dobilas, p20tl heru sukma cahyanto, p20cr Takashi Images, p21tr Creativa Images, p21cl Mirt Alexander, p24br Manamana, p26bl azmifile, p28bl Sony Herdiana, p28br Maharani afifah,p29tl edi alif, p29tr aditya_frzhm, p29bl Ryan Wijaya Ta, p30tc M Reza Faisal, p31tr Gunawan Kartapranata (https://commons.wikimedia.org/wiki/File:Garuda_Pancasila,_Coat_of_Arms_of_Indonesia.svg), p31ml Hebly Fauzan, p32 M Reza Faisal

NATIONAL LIBRARY OF AUSTRALIA
A catalogue record for this book is available from the National Library of Australia

CONTENTS

MAP OF INDONESIA

Mandala Suci Wenara Wana

BALI

Jakarta

JAVA

Fast Fact

The country exports 3,000 tons of frogs' legs to France annually.

Candi Borobudur
JAVA

Komodo Island
EAST NUSA TENGGARA

Gili Kedis Island
LOMBOK

SNAPSHOT

COUNTRY
Republic of Indonesia

CAPITAL
Jakarta

OFFICIAL LANGUAGE
Indonesian

AREA
1,919,440 square kilometres

POPULATION
281,358,622 (2023)

HIGHEST POINT Puncak Jaya, 4,884 metres

RELIGIONS Muslim, Buddhist, Christian, Hindu and Confucianism

CURRENCY Rp Indonesian rupiah

GOVERNMENT Unitary presidential constitutional republic

WELCOME TO INDONESIA

Indonesia, officially called the Republic of Indonesia, is located in Southeast Asia, with some territories in Oceania. It is the world's largest island country, with 17,508 islands, of which about 6,000 are inhabited. Indonesia is an archipelago of volcanoes, located within the Pacific Ring of Fire, and bordering a number of dangerous seismic faults.

Tarsius Tarsiers live in tropical forests

There is a constant risk of earthquakes, volcanic eruptions and tsunamis. The annual rainy season can also bring heavy rainfall and monsoon conditions that are amplified by deforestation, causing floods.

Dancer at Wakatobi Wave Festival in Southeast Sulawesi

The landscape of this fascinating country is as diverse as its people. There are over 300 ethnic groups in Indonesia, with 95 per cent being native Indonesian. Javanese is the largest ethnic group, accounting for approximately 40 per cent of the population. Apart from the Javanese, the other five largest ethnic groups are Sundanese, Batak, Sulawesi, Madurese, and Betawi.

Territories and Tensions

West Papaun tribesman in traditional costume

Four of Indonesia's islands are shared with other nations, causing tension in the region. Malaysia and Indonesia share two islands. Both countries share Sebatik off the coast of Kalimantan, while Borneo is shared between Indonesia, Malaysia and Brunei. Timor is divided between Indonesia and East Timor. The Western half of the Island of New Guinea, belongs to Indonesia and has two provinces known as Papua and West Papua, while the other eastern half of the island is known as Papua New Guinea or PNG.

Indonesia's Shared Islands:

1 Sebatik 2 Borneo 3 Timor 4 New Guinea

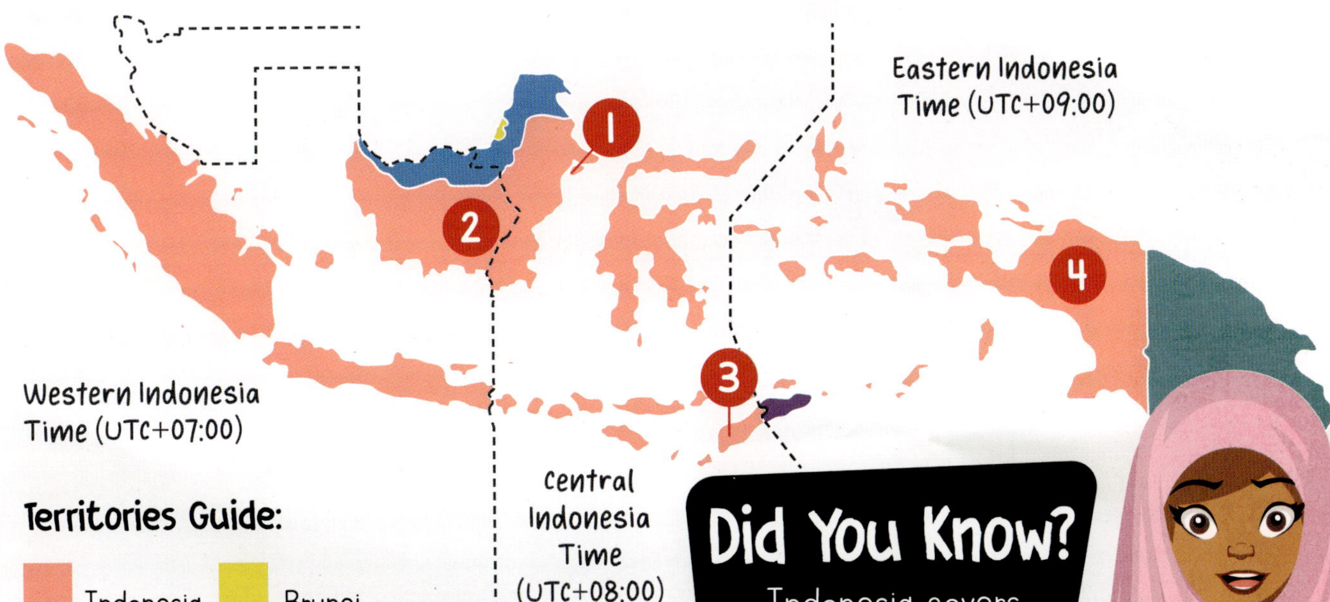

Territories Guide:

Indonesia, Brunei, Malaysia, East Timor, PNG

Did You Know?

Indonesia covers three time zones.

AT A GLANCE

Presidential Palace
WEST JAVA

Joko Widodo - President of Indonesia

Government

Indonesia is a multiparty republic, ruled by a president with primary executive power. The president and vice president are popularly elected to five-year terms.

Top Exports

Indonesia's top exports include coal products, palm oil, electronic equipment, gems and jewellery, petroleum and rubber.

Top Imports

Indonesia's top imports include oil, machinery, electronic equipment, iron, steel and plastics.

Nickel plant
SOROWAKO

Miner sieving and sorting tin

Natural Resources

Indonesia's natural resources include copper, nickel, timber, bauxite, gold and coal. Indonesia supplies 20 per cent of the world's tin.

Palm Oil

Tea

Cocoa

Important Agricultural Products

Indonesia is the world's largest producer of palm oil. Other important agricultural products include rubber, cocoa, coffee, tea, rice and tropical spices.

PEOPLE

Indonesia's main ethnic communities generally co-exist with very little disharmony. The country's motto is 'Unity in Diversity'.

Javanese

Javanese people are the largest ethnic group in Indonesia. Most Javanese still reside on Java however there has been some migration to other islands on the archipelago. Historically, most Javanese were Hindu, but today they follow a moderate form of Islam and less than 10 per cent follow orthodox Islam. A minority of Javanese are Buddhists, Hindus and Christians. Family life is central to Javanese society.

Sulawesi

Sulawesi is home to 208 ethnic subgroups. About 3.2 per cent of the total population live in Sulawesi.

Girl wearing traditional Kaili Tribe clothes, typical of central Sulawesi

Malay

About five million Malays live in Indonesia, making it the largest Malay population outside Malaysia. Indonesian is derived from the Malay language.

Sundanese

Sundanese people make up 16 per cent of the population and generally live in the provinces of West Java, Jakarta and Banten.

Chinese

The Chinese are a small but significant ethnic group in Indonesia, most of them descendants of families that have lived in the country for generations. Chinese are prominent in Indonesia's business world and despite being a small minority, more than half of the top twenty wealthiest Indonesian businessmen are ethnic Chinese.

Say what?

A number of Indonesian ethnic groups have a reputation for some spine-tingling practices.

Zombies

The Toraja from Sulawesi have unusual funeral rights that can often take place over a period of years, and include dressing the corpse and having it stand up. Photos of this unusual practice went viral around the internet a few years ago and had some people questioning whether zombies existed. That mystery was debunked when the funeral rituals of Toraja were explained.

Rock-cut family tombs at Lo'ko' Mata, Tana Toraja, Sulawesi

Headhunters

The Dayaks are the indigenous people of Indonesian Borneo (Kalimantan), as well as Malaysian Borneo and Brunei. Many Dayak live in longhouses and farm rice, but what they are really famous for is the practice of headhunting. Nowadays visitors are at risk of losing their heads over the beauty of the region. Actual headhunting doesn't happen anymore.

DAILY LIFE

Daily life varies in Indonesia with poverty playing a major role for many people. While living standards are improving for many Indonesians, over half the population still lives on less than two dollars a day. Many rural areas lack basic services and the need to work drives many people to the cities, where overcrowding is a problem.

Family Life

Family is the foundation of life in Indonesia. Children are often looked after by their grandparents while their parents work.

EDUCATION

School is compulsory for 9 years. Indonesian children start school at the age of six and spend six years in primary school and three years in high school. In recent years more students have been choosing to complete the extra three years of high school, in order to go on to university or further study. Young children may speak their regional language at school, until year three when classes are taught in Indonesian.

LIFE IN CITIES

Indonesia's cities are bursting at the seams with the constant influx of people who are looking for work. By 2025 it is expected that 68 per cent of Indonesia's population will live in cities. Despite this trend, not enough money is being spent on infrastructure and less than half of households have access to safe water, with only two per cent of people living in cities having access to proper sanitation systems.

Over thirty million people live in slums. Other city dwellers live in apartments, often with many other family members. It's not unusual for three generations of a family to live in one small apartment.

LIFE IN RURAL AREAS

Farming is the main occupation for Indonesians in rural areas. Many people live below the poverty line often without access to basic sanitation and safe water. Another major problem is natural disasters.

Homes in rural areas display ethnic and religious influences in the architecture. They are often made of wood with bamboo walls and tiled, wooden or dried palm fibre roofs. Villages around Indonesia vary, with some maintaining community longhouses, while others have newer single-family homes. In Bali, walled family complexes are common.

TRADITIONAL CLOTHING

Batak woman holding a traditionally woven 'Ulos' cloth

Today, most Indonesians wear western style clothing when they are out and at work, but at home many relax in a sarong. Batik cloth is used for sarongs, but also for shirts for men and blouses for women. Many Muslim women wear a headscarf called a kerudung.

The kebaya is a traditional blouse dress for women. Although it is recognised as the national costume it is worn more by women in Bali and Java. For men, the peci is a traditional cap approved as the national headdress.

LANGUAGE

There are more than 700 languages spoken in Indonesia. The official language is Indonesian, also known as Bahasa Indonesia. Around 40 million people are native speakers, and about 200 million people speak it as a second language.

Speak Bahasa Indonesia

Terima kasih
Thank you

Selamat pagi
Good morning

Tolong
Please

Did You Know?
Bahasa Indonesia is a different dialect of Malay, the language in Malaysia

Apa kabar?
How are you?

Selamat siang
Good afternoon

Saya tidak mengerti
I don't understand

Selamat malam
Goodnight

RELIGION

Indonesia's government recognises six religions: Islam, Hinduism, Protestantism, Catholicism, Buddhism and Confucianism. All citizens must follow of one of these religions.

Hubbul Wathan Mosque - West Nusa Tenggara Islamic Center

Islam

Islam is practised by nearly 88 per cent of all Indonesians. It is the world's largest Muslim population. There are many beautiful mosques in Indonesia, including the Istiqlal Mosque in Jakarta, which is the largest mosque in Southeast Asia. Muslims pray five times a day and they observe a holy day, each week, on Fridays.

Ramadan

Ramadan is the most important event on the Islamic calendar. Ramadan is a month of fasting during daylight hours to display faith to Allah. At the end of the Ramadan month, families and friends celebrate together with the Eid-Al-Fitr feast.

Galungan

This is an ancestor worship festival celebrated on the island of Bali. People travel home to their families to make offerings and pay respects.

Buddhist monks carrying out the pindapata tradition, in Magelang

Buddhism

Buddhism arrived in Indonesia in the 2nd century and over the following centuries many incredible temples were built. By the late 15th century, Islam was the dominant religion and now less than one per cent of the population is Buddhist.

Hinduism

Hinduism is practiced by less than two per cent of the total population, but in Bali over 83 per cent of Indonesians are Hindu.

Fast Fact

The most important national festival is Independence Day, which is held on August 17 every year.

Christianity

Christianity is Indonesia's second largest religion, with 24 million followers, or 10 per cent of the population. Two branches of Christianity are officially recognised: Protestant and Roman Catholic.

Christian church onthe island of Arborek, West Papua

KEY MOMENTS IN HISTORY

Early Kingdoms

Around 400 AD, Hinduism arrived and great empires were built. The Hindu Sailendra and Mataram dynasties ruled Central Java while the Buddhist Srivijaya kingdom ruled Sumatra. Trade routes developed in the area and Arab traders began arriving. By 1520 Java was completely converted to Islam.

The history of human settlement in Indonesia can be traced back thousands of years. Around two million to 500,000 years ago human ancestors known as Homo erectus, or Java Man, lived in the region.

Portrait of a senior merchant of the Dutch East India Company with his wife

Colonial Rule

In the early 1500s the Dutch, English, Spanish and Portuguese colonial powers were battling it out for the region. Indonesia was then known as the Spice Islands. From 1611 the Dutch East India Company (VOC) established their headquarters in Batvia, now Jakarta, and built a series of ports. The colonised region became known as the Dutch East Indies.

Independence

The Japanese occupied the area during the Second World War. This weakened Dutch rule. Following the Japanese surrender in August 1945, Indonesian nationalist, Soekarno (Sukarno) declared the independent, Republic of Indonesia. The Netherlands fought back but international pressure forced the Dutch to concede independence in 1949. Sukarno was president for 21 years, until Suharto came to power in 1967.

MONAS is Indonesia's National Monument, representing their struggle for independence

Suharto Years

General Suharto's thirty-year authoritarian rule began with a purging of anyone suspected to be communist. Thousands of people were killed or went missing. Although life improved for many Indonesians, corruption was rife. Suharto's closest allies became extremely wealthy during his rule, while anyone who challenged him was crushed.

Recent Times

Democratic processes were strengthened with the country's first direct presidential election, won by Susilo Bambang Yudhoyono in 2004. In more recent years, the economy has performed strongly and the standard of living has improved. In 2014, Joko Widodo became the first directly elected president without ties to the military and political elite.

FOOD

A wide range of factors have influenced Indonesian cuisine. Early traders and colonists brought new spices and dishes that began blending with regional foods and traditional recipes.

Boiled rice is a staple food and ingredients such as cloves, nutmeg, chilli, lime and peanuts are common. Chinese dishes such as spring rolls and noodles are now completely integrated into local cuisine. Sumatra has gulai, a local adaptation of an Indian curry. Javanese cuisine is broken into three regional sub-groups but all tend to be simpler than their Sumatran neighbours.

Hinduism influences Balinese food, so beef isn't traditionally used.

Some dishes, such as Nasi Goreng, are so popular that they are found right across the country and are considered to be national dishes.

Fabulous Fruit

Indonesia's climate is well suited to growing tropical fruit and you will find a wide variety of familiar and not so familiar fruits all over the country. The strong-smelling durian is so popular that there are now durian sweets, durian soup and durian ice cream. The rambutan is another favourite. The rambutan has a hairy appearance and can be eaten straight from the tree.

Rambutan fruit

ON THE MENU

Nasi Goreng

Nasi goreng means fried rice, and includes ingredients such as soy sauce, shrimp paste, chilli pepper, spring onions, turmeric, nutmeg, ginger, garlic paste, shallots and garlic, mixed into pre-cooked rice and chicken, shrimp or beef and egg.

Satay

Small pieces of chicken, beef or pork on wooden sticks, covered in a peanut sauce.

Gado Gado

Sold throughout Indonesia, but with some regional differences, gado gado is a vegetable salad served with peanut sauce and boiled egg.

Mie Goreng

This is a spicy fried noodle dish with shallots, cabbage and prawn, chicken or beef.

MAJOR SITES

The sheer size and diversity of Indonesia, its stunning beauty, beaches, dive spots and forests, means it is one of the world's growing tourist destinations.

Komodo dragon on Rinca Island

Komodo National Park

Located in the centre of the Indonesian archipelago, Komodo National Park consists of a number of islands, including Komodo, Rinca and Padar. They are well known for their incredible dive sites, but the main claim to fame for these islands is that they are home to the famous Komodo dragon. The Komodo is the largest living species of lizard and can grow up to three metres in length.

Borobudur Temple

Borobudur temple on Java is the world's biggest Buddhist temple. Completed in the 9th century, it was rediscovered in 1815 buried under volcanic ash.

Bali

Bali is an island situated between Java and Lombok. It is also a province that includes not only the main island but a few smaller ones as well. Bali has a tropical monsoon climate, with pleasant temperatures between 20 and 33 degrees Celsius. The rainy season is between October and March.

Bali has a population of about 4.5 million people. The majority of the population is Hindu with smaller communities of Muslims, Christians and Buddhists. Most Balinese speak Indonesian and Balinese. Life in Bali can be at a slower pace. Multi-generational families share walled compounds, often containing numerous homes and a shrine. Many people work in professions that haven't changed much for generations.

Farming, fishing and craftsmanship are still dominant professions, however the tourism industry is booming and opening up career paths for younger generations.

Kalimantan Borneo

Borneo is divided among three countries: Malaysia, Brunei and Indonesia. Indonesia's region is known as Kalimantan and consists of 73 per cent of the island. Borneo is believed to have the highest plant diversity of any region on earth. The world's largest flower, the Rafflesia, is found on Borneo. It is also home to thousands of bird and insect species, many of which aren't found anywhere else. Borneo's most famous residents are the orangutans and Sunda clouded leopards.

Orangutan in Kalimantan Borneo

GEOGRAPHY AND CLIMATE

Indonesia is the world's largest archipelago, made up of 17,508 islands. Four of the islands are shared with other countries. Situated in the Pacific Ring of Fire, Indonesia is a rich mix of volcanoes, coral reefs and coastal plains. About two-thirds of the country is covered in rainforests. The volcanic ash from Indonesia's volcanoes has made for fertile soil.

Mount Jayawijaya, Papau

Mountain Ranges

Most of Indonesia's islands are mountainous. Jayawijaya Mountains and the Sudirman Mountains in Irian Jaya reach between 4,700 and 5,000 meters in height. The highest peak is Puncak Jaya in the Sudirman Mountains, reaching 4,884 meters.

Climate

Indonesia is situated near the equator and has a tropical climate. Instead of four seasons it has two: a wet season from November to March and a dry season from June to October.

Mount Krakatoa erupting

Sumatran Tiger

Volcanic Eruptions

Indonesia has more active volcanoes than any other country in the world. In August 1883 Mt Krakatoa exploded, plunging everything into darkness within a 250-kilometre radius. The explosion caused a tsunami that killed 36,000 people and washed away 165 villages. Even today, Krakatoa is one of the world's most famous eruptions. Now, modern day satellite technology helps identify a potential emergency and enables Indonesian officials to evacuate those nearby.

Islands

Indonesia has 54,716 kilometres of coastline. Many islands have been formed through volcanic activity while some are coral atolls.

Wildlife at Risk

Indonesia has a diverse array of wildlife and some species cannot be found anywhere else in the world. The country's rainforests are biologically and culturally rich, and home to nearly 15 per cent of all known species of plants, mammals and birds on earth. Sadly, this is under threat due to mass deforestation caused by the palm oil and paper industries. Deforestation poses a grave threat to the environment due to loss of species and the impact on climate change. Many environmental groups are working to change policies and practices that are contributing to deforestation.

Here are five animals that are only found in Indonesia. Can you find out if they are at risk?

- Orangutan
- Javan Rhinoceros
- Sumatran Tiger
- Tarsius Tarsier
- Komodo Dragon

TRANSPORT

Being an archipelago, maritime transport has been important to Indonesia for centuries. Boats and Ferries are essential to carry people, cargo and vehicles from island to island. Trucks are the major method for transporting goods around the country. Traffic congestion in cities is a major problem. Because of this, there are some unusual methods of getting around.

Getek: Many Jakartans travel using traditional bamboo rafts called geteks

Ojek: These taxi-bikes are used instead of cars to transport paying passengers

Delman or Andong: The horse and carriage is being phased out but are still spotted occasionally in Jakarta

Becak: These two-seater tricycle rickshaws were banned from Jakarta, but can still be found in smaller cities and towns

Pinisi: Traditional two-masted sailing boats used to transport people and cargo between islands

Bajaj: These motorised rickshaws are usually orange and can fit up to five passengers

FLAG, SYMBOLS AND EMBLEMS

Flag of Indonesia

The National Flag consists of two equal horizontal sections of red above white. The flag was adopted on August 17, 1945, after Indonesia became independent from The Netherlands.

The Indonesian flag is very similar to two other flags. Can you pick it below? The Indonesian flag is in the centre. It is longer than the Flag of Monaco at the top, and the colours are flipped on the Polish flag at the bottom.

Coat of Arms

Indonesia's coat of arms is the Garuda Pancasila, composed of a Garuda, a large mythical bird, and heraldic shield.

National Anthem

Indonesia's national anthem is Indonesia Raya.

National Animal

Indonesia's national animal is the Komodo dragon.

GLOSSARY

archipelago group of islands

climate change shift in the planet's weather and climate patterns

colonialism control or governing influence of one nation over another country, territory or people

culture practices, beliefs and customs of a society or people

deforestation clearing of trees in an unsustainable way

endangered when a species is at risk

ethnic from a different culture or country

independence when a country is ruled by its own people

Pacific Ring of Fire geographical area in the Pacific Ocean where earthquakes and volcanoes are common

sustainability ability to continue for a long time

tropical hot, humid climate

typhoon powerful tropical storm

INDEX